D1607289

Bear's *Adventure*

in Alphabet Town

by Janet McDonnell
illustrated by Linda Hohag

created by Wing Park Publishers

CP CHILDRENS PRESS ®
CHICAGO

Library of Congress Cataloging-in-Publication Data

McDonnell, Janet, 1962-
    Bear's adventure in Alphabet Town / by Janet McDonnell ;
illustrated by Linda Hohag.
       p.   cm. — (Read around Alphabet Town)
    Summary: Bear meets a lot of "b" words on her adventure in
Alphabet Town. Includes activities.
    ISBN 0-516-05402-3
    [1. Alphabet—Fiction. 2. Bears—Fiction.] I. Hohag, Linda,
ill. II. Title. III. Series.
PZ7.M478436Be   1992
[E]—dc 20   91-20543
                                 CIP
                                 AC

Bear's *Adventure*

in Alphabet Town

You are now entering Alphabet Town,
With letters from "A" to "Z."
I'm going on a "B" adventure today,
So come along with me.

This is the "B" house of Alphabet
Town. A big bear lives here.

Bear likes everything that begins
with the letter "b."

But most of all, Bear loves

birthday parties.

One day, Bear's friend Beaver sent him a note. It said:

Bear was so happy. "I will give Beaver the best gift of all," he said. And off he went.

First, he bought a beautiful

basket.

Then he filled the basket with

blueberries and bark.

When the basket was full, Bear tied a pretty

blue
bow

on it. "Beaver will love this present," said Bear.

And he bounced down the path to
Beaver's birthday party. On the way,
Bear saw a big, beautiful blueberry.

It was better than any of the berries
in the basket. So Bear put down the
basket to pick the big blueberry.

Just then a

bird

flew down and picked up the basket
in her beak.

Off she flew with the basket to
a nearby

branch.

"You bad bird!" cried Bear. "Give me my basket."

"It is my basket now," said the bird.

"I will trade you," said Bear.
"I will give you my

bubble gum

if you will give me the basket."
"No," said the bird. "Bubble gum
gets stuck in my beak."

"Then," said Bear, "I will bake you some

brownies

if you will give me the basket."
"No," said the bird. "I like berries much better than brownies."

Now bear was upset. "What will
I do?" he cried. Then he had an
idea. He ran home.

Soon he came back with a

balloon.

He hid under the branch where
the bird was.

And he began to blow up the balloon.

It grew bigger and bigger and bigger.

Then Bear broke the balloon with a

BANG!

The bird was so scared, she dropped
the birthday basket.

Bear grabbed the basket. He ran
all the way to Beaver's house.

By the time Bear got there, he was
all out of breath.

"Happy Birthday, Beaver," he said.

"Oh, Bear," said Beaver. "This is
the best birthday gift ever."
And he gave his friend a big bear hug.

MORE FUN WITH BEAR

What's in a Name?

In my "b" adventure, you read many "b" words. My name begins with "B." Many of my friends' names begin with "B" too. Here are a few.

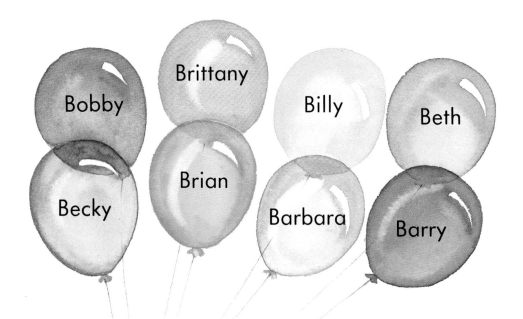

Do you know other names that start with "B"? Does your name start with "B"?

Bear's Word Hunt

I like to hunt for "b" words.
Can you help me find the words
on this page that begin with
"b"? How many are there? Can
you read them?

bows

ball

robin

football

kitten

crib

books

cab

Can you find any words with "b" in the middle?
Can you find any words with "b" at the end?
Can you find a word with no "b"?

Bear's Favorite Things

"B" is my favorite letter. Can you guess why? I love "b" things. You can find some of my favorite "b" things in my house on page 7. How many "b" things can you find there? Can you think of more "b" things?

Now you make up a "b" adventure.